The 1-Day Breakout Method

By

Pacific Trading Systems Research

Edited by Eddie Kwong

Pacific Trading Systems Research

Los Angeles, California

ISBN 0-9721229-0-7

Printed in the United States of America

Disclaimer

Table of Contents

Part One
Introduction

One of the things that chew many traders up is that they trade in trend-less, sideways markets. The biggest gains come from either climbing aboard trends or catching large reversals. And when you have a strategy that does both, then the chances for quick, large moves are greatly improved. This is what the 1-Day Breakout Method (ODBM) does.

The ODBM is a four-day pattern that trades strongly trending markets. It looks for markets to break out, have a one-day move in the opposite direction, and then experience a pause day. The day after the pause day, you will climb aboard if the original strong trend resumes. This method is conceptually like many other trend pullback methods including Dave Landry's Trend Knockout, found in *Dave Landry on Swing Trading*. **The methodology you will learn has historically been profitable up to 75% of the time within one day with specific sectors and stocks.**

Now before looking at the method and the statistics that show how well the ODBM works, let's quickly talk about trading this method. Even though we'll show you the statistical edge that has been achieved with a mechanical entry and exit, we are not encouraging you to trade it this way. It is only being used to show you what it has done over the past decade. The better way to trade this is to exit using some discretion. How you do this is up to you. But the main thing is to climb aboard these rapidly moving stocks and markets, use tight protective stops and let the profits run when they occur.

Part Two
The Trend

The single most important reason this method works is because of the trend. The price pattern you will learn is secondary to the trend. Here, we will teach you how to find the best trends to trade this method.

There are two ways to trade the ODBM. One is with a 20-day new high and a 20-day new low. The other is with ADX. ADX is a bit more complicated, so let's look at it first.

What is ADX?

ADX is simply a measurement of the strength of the trend. The stronger the trend, the higher the ADX reading. Readings above 25 signify strong trends. In extreme markets you will see ADX readings as high as 50 and 60. There are many different periods of ADX you can use, and we use the

14-period ADX (this is the likely default reading in your software package).

The second (and last) part of ADX is the +DI/-DI component. ADX only measures the strength of the trend. It does not measure the direction of the trend. The +DI/-DI reading does. If the trend is up, the +DI reading will be higher than the -DI reading. If the trend is down, the -DI reading will be higher than the +DI reading. A strong up-trending market will have an ADX reading above 25 and a +DI reading above its -DI reading. A strongly down-trending market will have an ADX reading above 25 and a -DI reading higher than its +DI reading. This is it! The math for ADX can be very complicated, but it is not necessary to know. The important thing is to understand what the ADX means and how to read it. And with the information just presented, you now have it.

Here are two examples of trending markets with high ADX readings. As you can see, the first example shows a market with a high ADX and a +DI greater than its -DI. This tells us the trend is strongly up. The second example is a market with a high ADX with its -DI greater than its +DI. This tells us the trend is strongly down.

Example A — Example of an Uptrending Market with ADX, +DI, and -DI Indicators

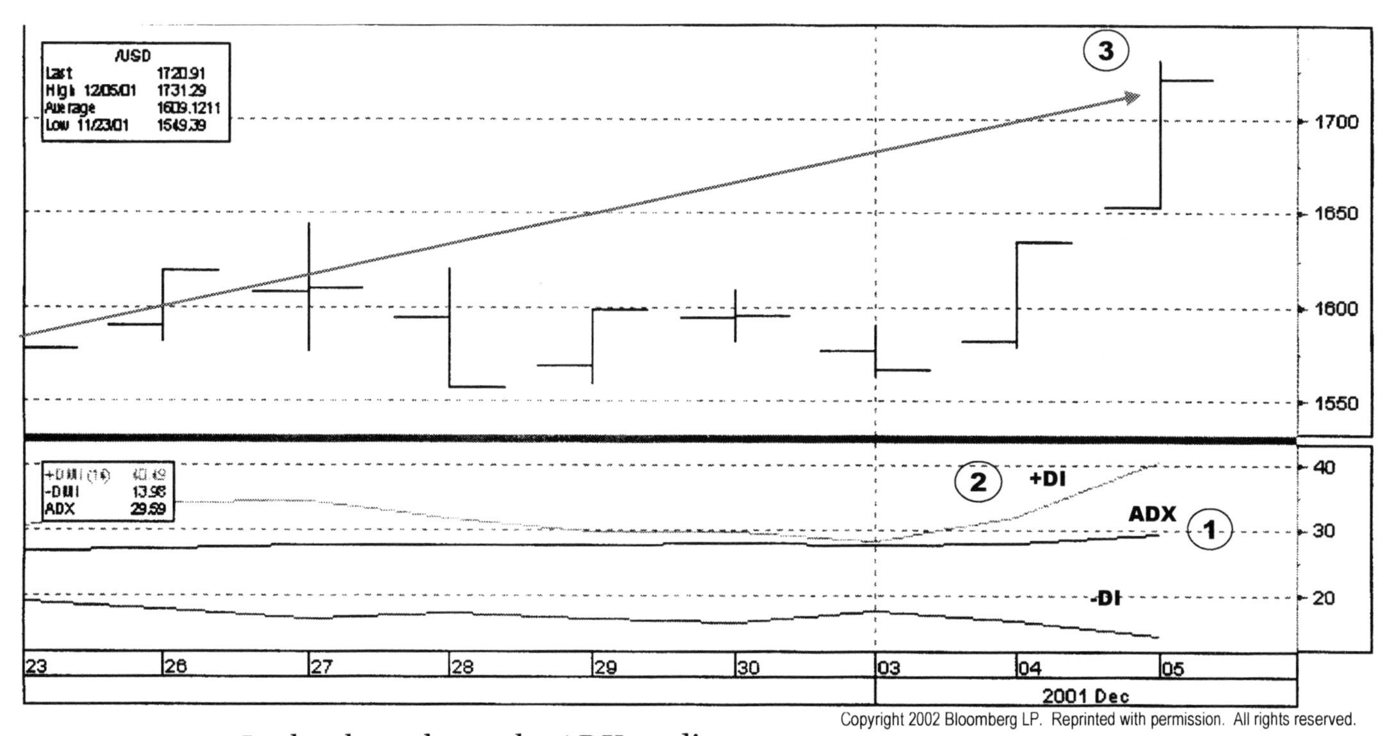

1. In the chart above, the ADX reading on 12/5/01 is at approximately 30, indicating a **strongly trending market**.

2. From 11/23/01 through 12/5/01, the +DI line is above the -DI line which indicates that the S&P 500 Index is in a **uptrend**.

3. As you can tell from this chart, the S&P 500 Index trended up to approximately 1720 from about 1575 over the course of eight trading days.

Example B — Example of a Downtrending Market with ADX, +DI, and -DI

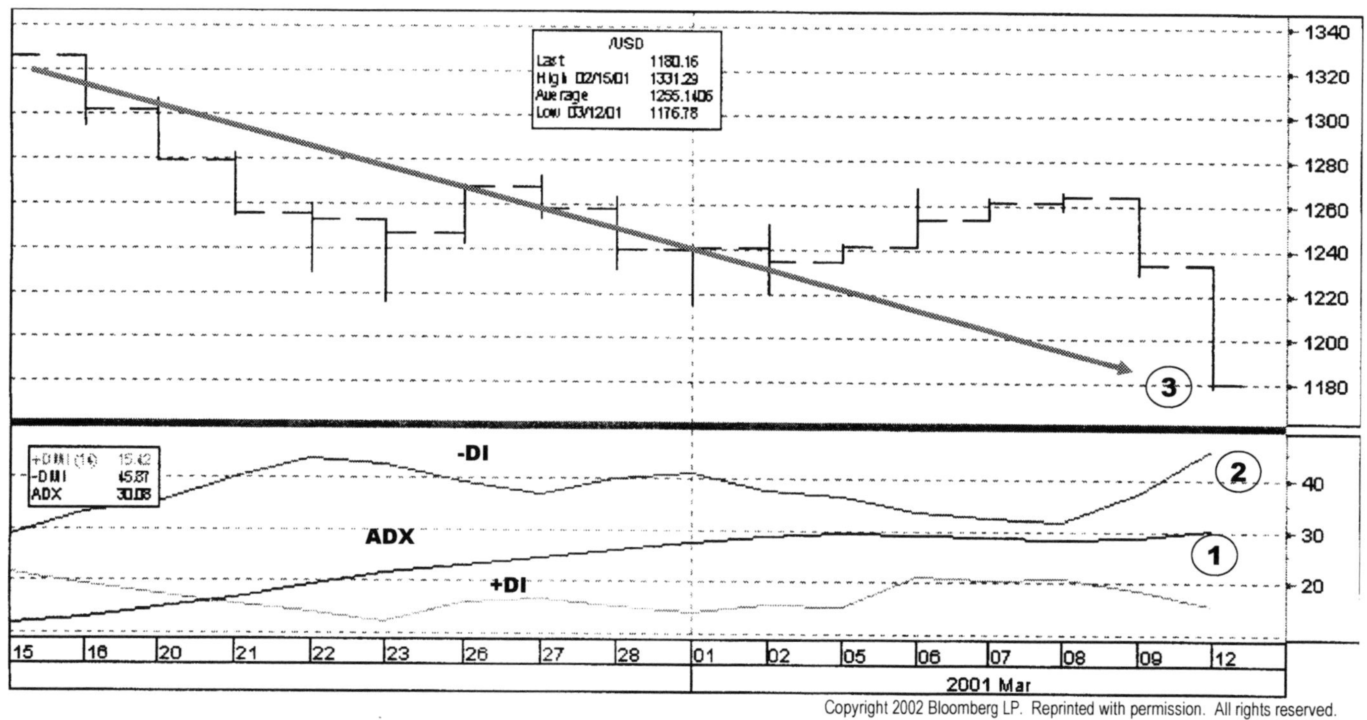

1. As you can see in the chart above, the ADX on 3/12/01 is at 30 indicating a **strongly trending market**.

2. Also from 2/15/01 through 3/12/01, the -DI is well above the +DI which indicates that the S&P 500 Index is in a **downtrend**.

3. As you can tell from this chart, the S&P 500 Index has trended down to 1180 from about 1330 over the course of a month.

For the ODBM, you will be buying markets and stocks whose ADX is 25 or greater and whose +DI is greater than its -DI. You will be shorting markets and stocks whose ADX is 25 or greater and whose -DI is greater than its +DI.

New 20-day Highs, New 20-day Lows

The second way to trade the ODBM is with stocks and sectors making new 20-day highs or new 20-day lows. Simply find those markets that make a 20-day high or low today. The day they do this is the first day of the four-day setup.

Next is an example of a stock making a 20-day high.

Example C — Example of an Uptrending Market using 20-day New Highs, Applied Materials (AMAT)

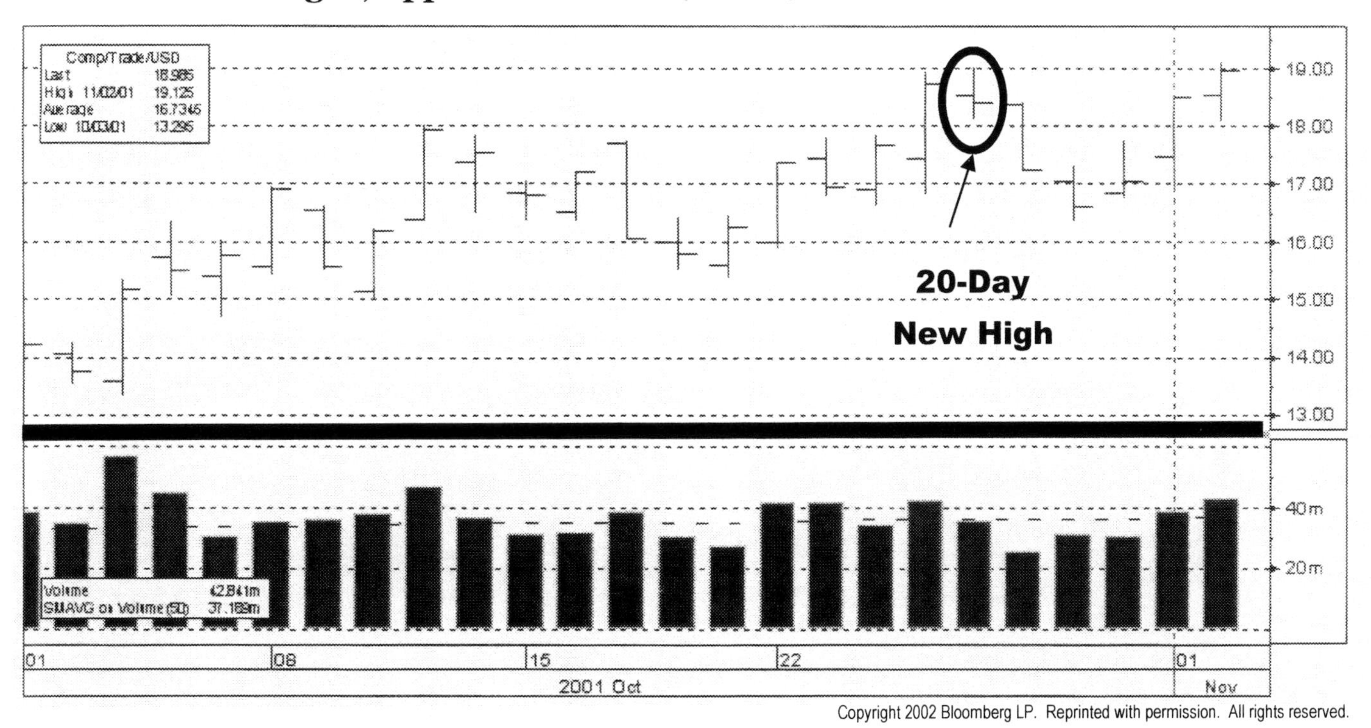

Next is an example of a stock making a 20-day low.

Example D — Example of a Downtrending Market using 20-day New Lows, America Online (AOL)

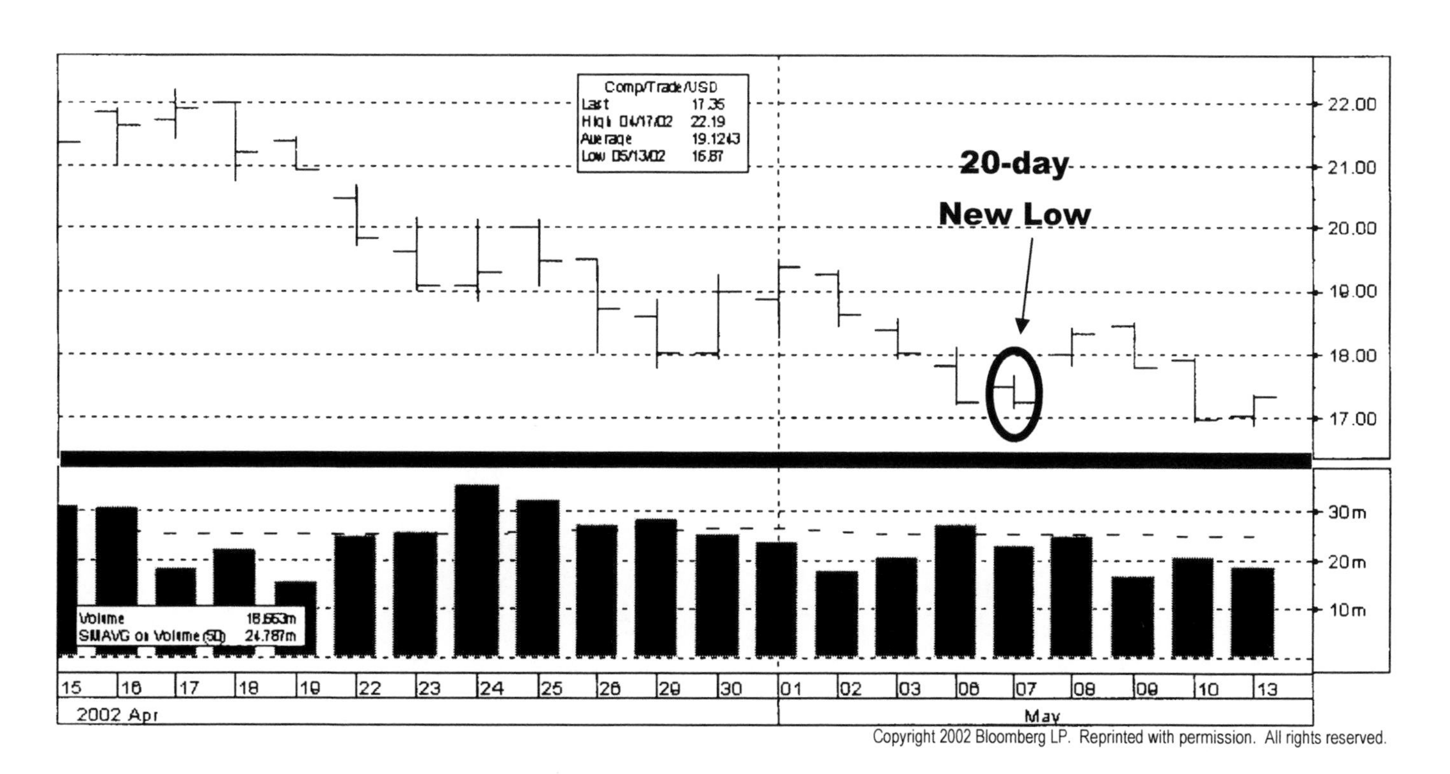

Now let's move on to the ODBM pattern.

The Pattern

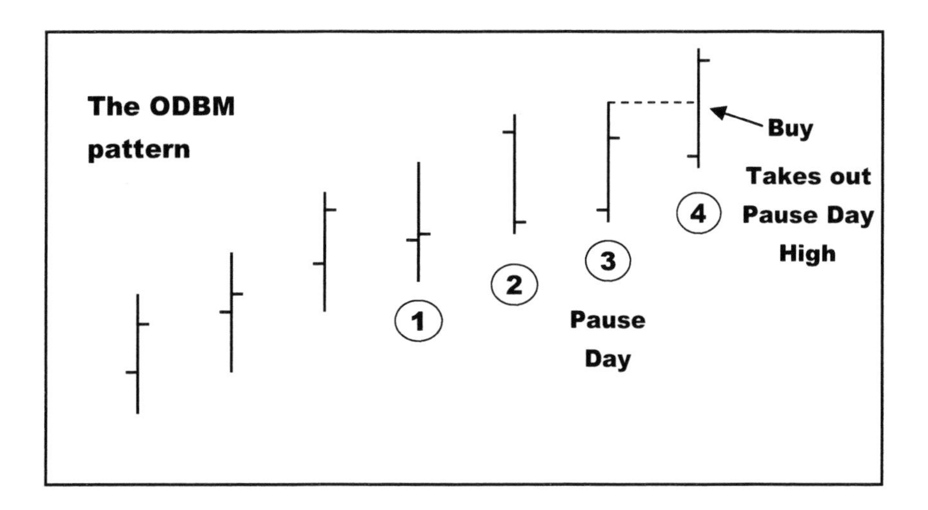

The pattern is very simple. It looks like this for buys:

1. The market makes a new 20-day high (or using ADX, the ADX is greater than 25 and the +DI is greater than the -DI).

2. **The Setup Day**: In an uptrending market (identified with either ADX or a 20-day new high), you will wait for a market or stock to close in the **bottom 25% of its range**.

3. **The Pause Day**: The next day is the pause day.

4. **The Trigger Day**: The next day, after the pause day (only), buy if the market reaches the pause day's high. The buy should be **just above the pause day's high**.
5. Exit is discretionary, and we'll talk about it in a later section.

For sells (short sells) the market looks like this:

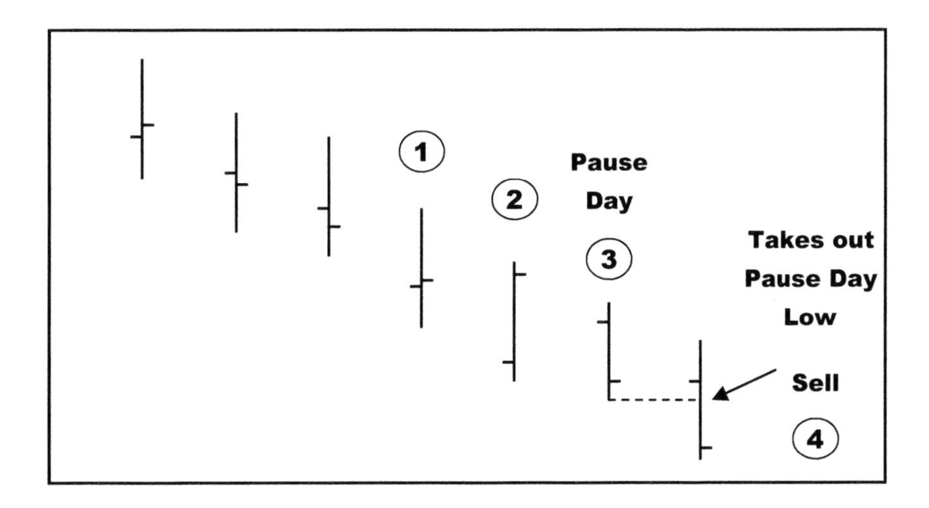

1. A 20-day new low (or the ADX is greater than 25 and the -DI is greater than the +DI).
2. **The Setup Day**: In a downtrending market (as identified by ADX or a new 20-day low), wait for a close in the **top 25% of its range.**

3. **The Pause Day**

4. **The Trigger Day**: The next day, after the pause day (only), sell short **just below the pause day's low**.

5. Exit is again discretionary.

Let's look at some examples using ADX. Then we'll look at a few examples using new highs and new lows.

Example 1 — Nasdaq 100 Index

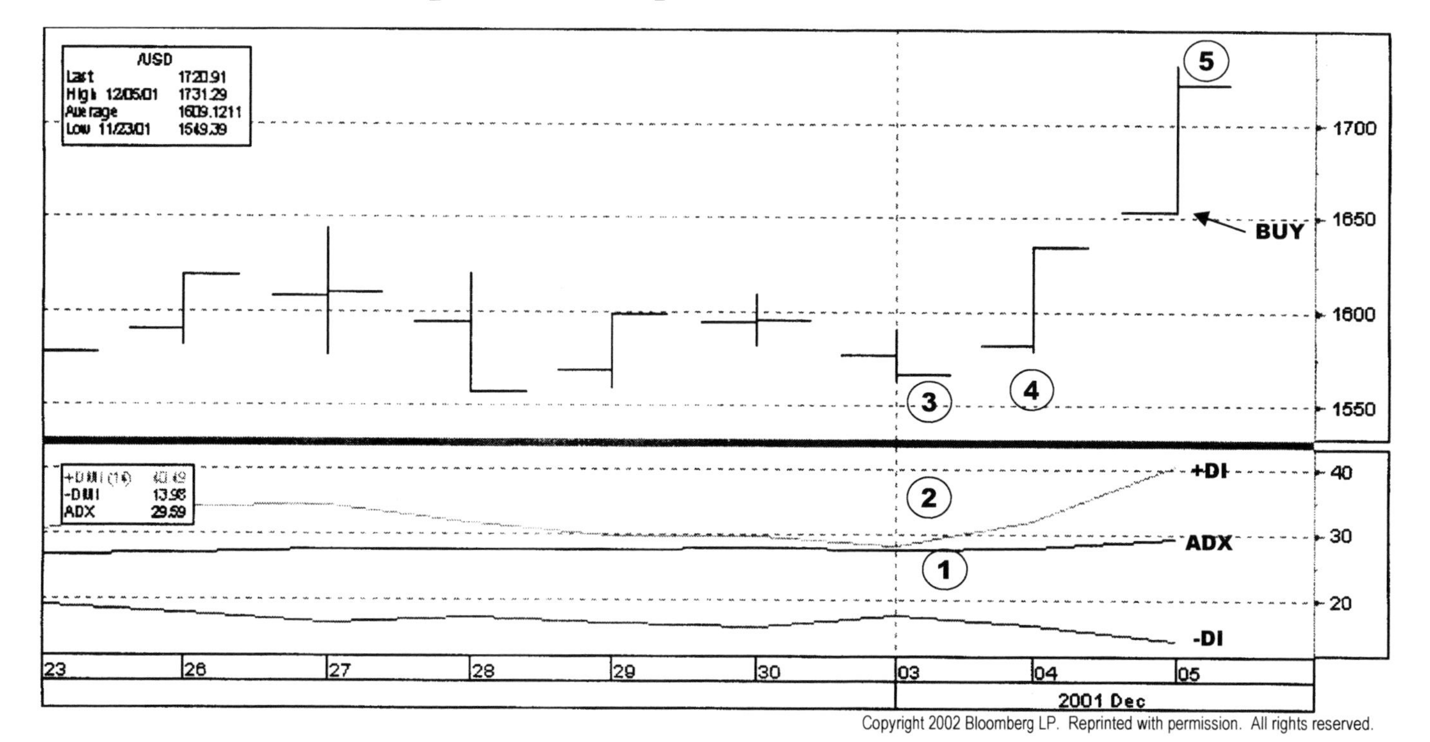

1. ADX is greater than 25.

2. +DI is greater than -DI, signifying the trend is up.

3. A close in the bottom 25% of the range.

4. Pause day (in this case, it was a resumption of the trend – a good sign).

5. Buy on the opening as the market trades above yesterday's high, and the NDX explodes 67 points.

Example 2 — S&P Index

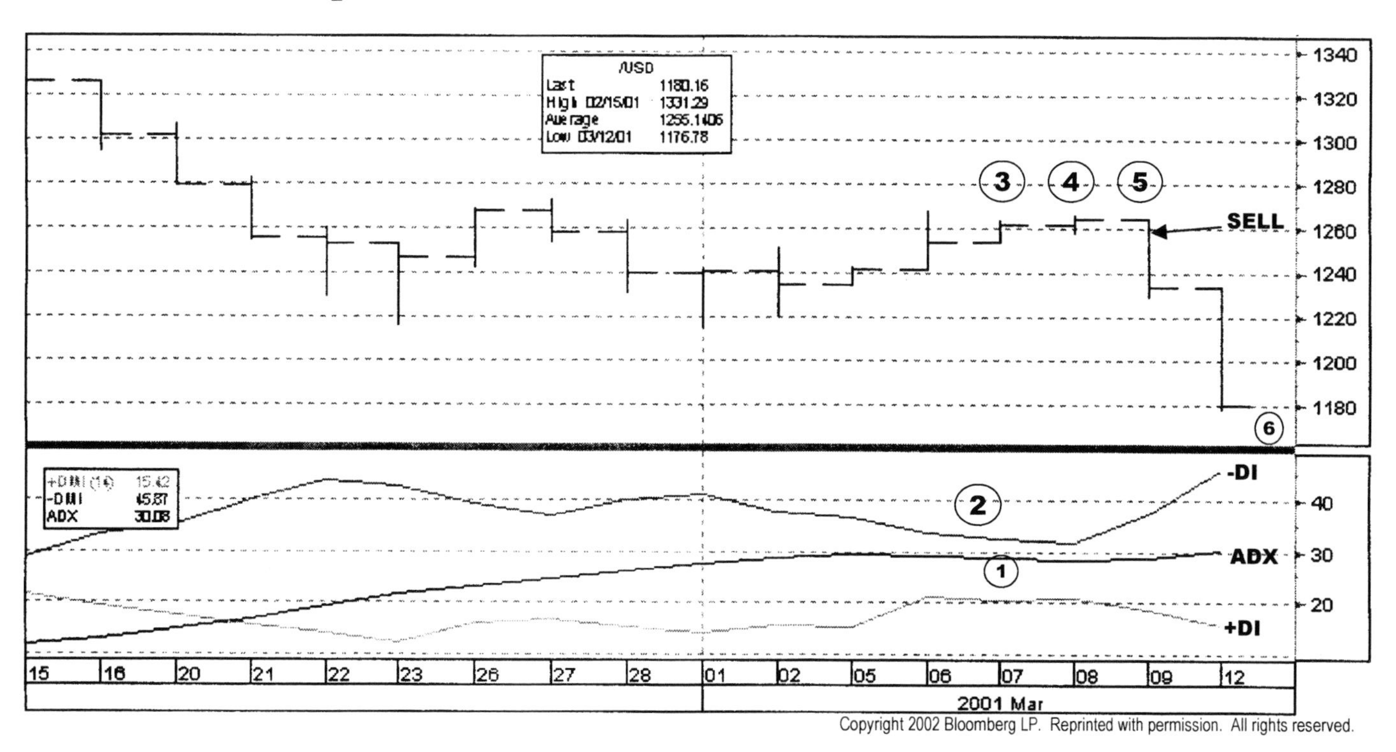

1. The ADX is above 25, signifying a strong trend.
2. The -DI is greater than the +DI, signifying the trend is down.
3. A close in the top 25% of the range.
4. The pause day.
5. The market trades under the pause day low, and we go short at 1257.60.
6. The market collapses and closes 77 points lower in a day.

Example 3 — Securities Broker Dealer Index (XBD)

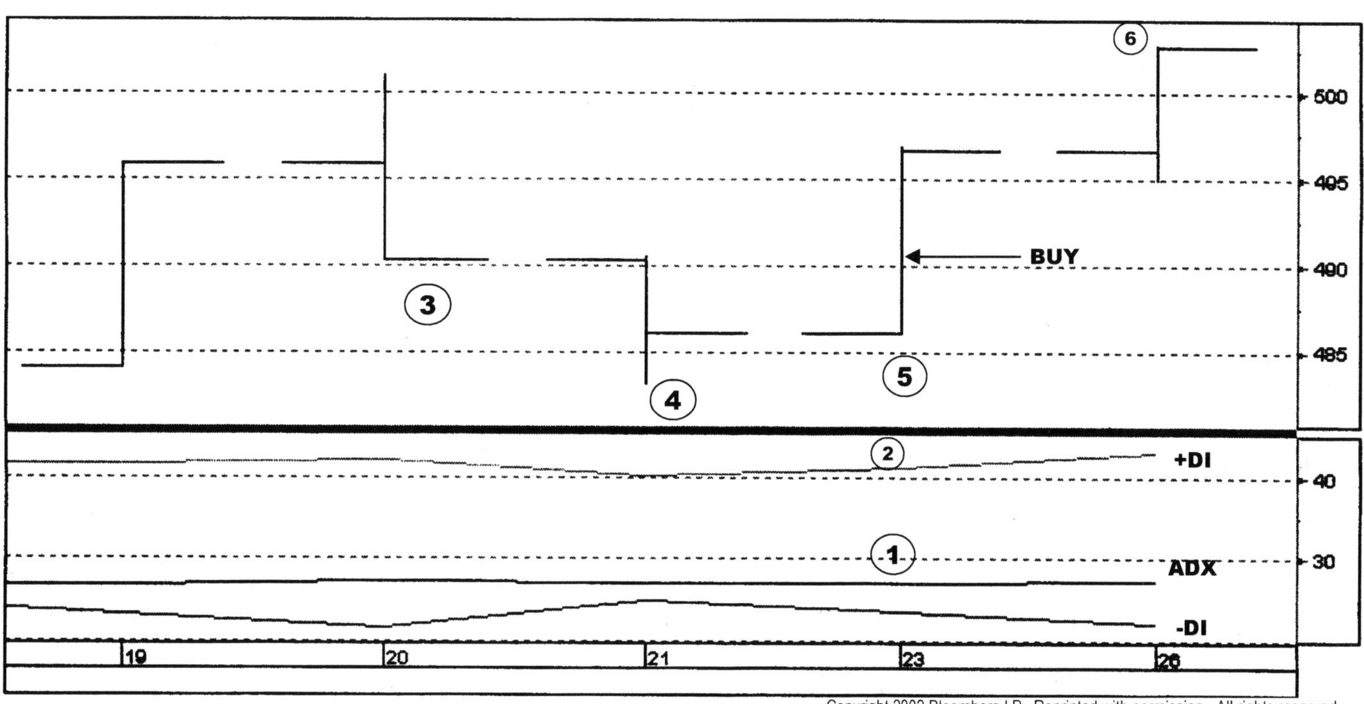

Here is an example with the Brokerage Index.

1. ADX is greater than 25.
2. +DI is greater than -DI, telling us it's an uptrend.
3. The close is in the bottom of the range.
4. Pause day.
5. Buy just above the pause day high.
6. A 2.5% move in a day.

Example 4 — Nasdaq 100 Index

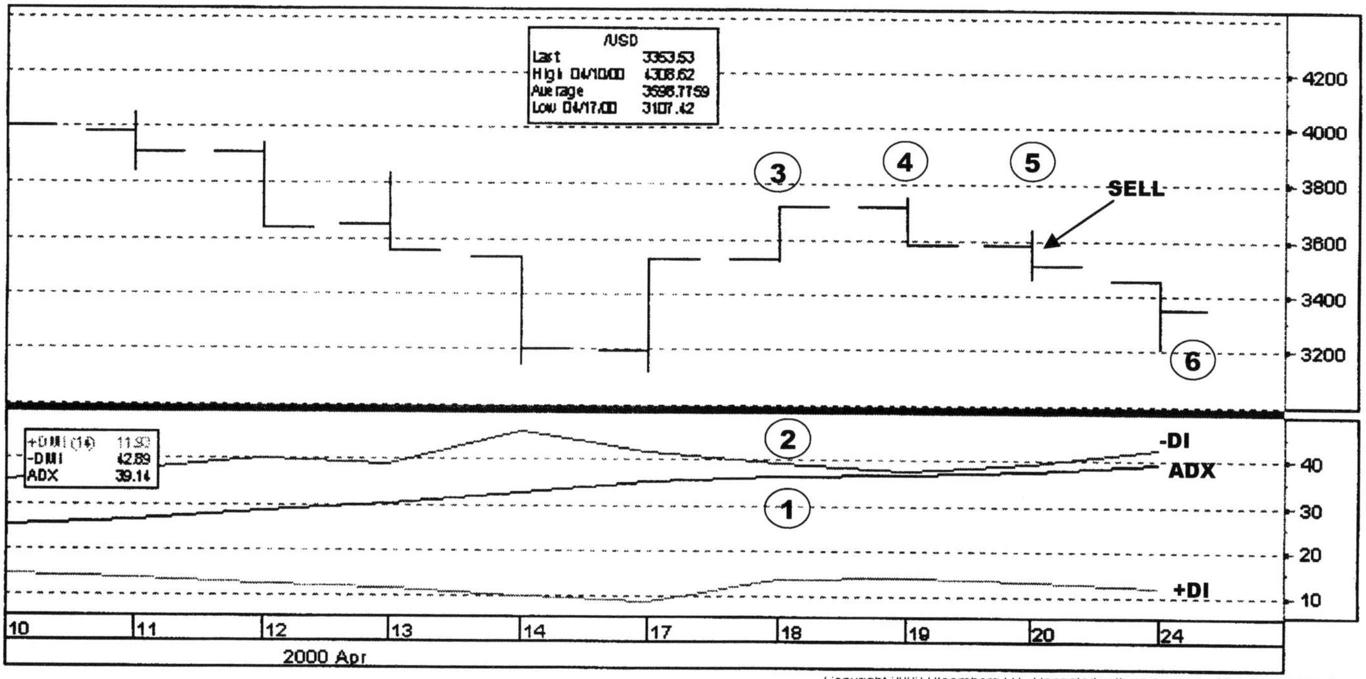

Here's an example of what can happen when you find a market that has gone crazy.

1. ADX is above 25.
2. Downtrend market as measured by the -DI reading above the +DI.
3. Close in the top of the range.
4. Pause day.
5. Takes out the pause day's low, and we go short at 3578.
6. The market incredibly loses as much as 10% of its value intraday the next day. Again, this is rare, but it shows the importance of finding these volatile markets.

Example 5 — PHLX Semiconductor Sector Index (SOX)

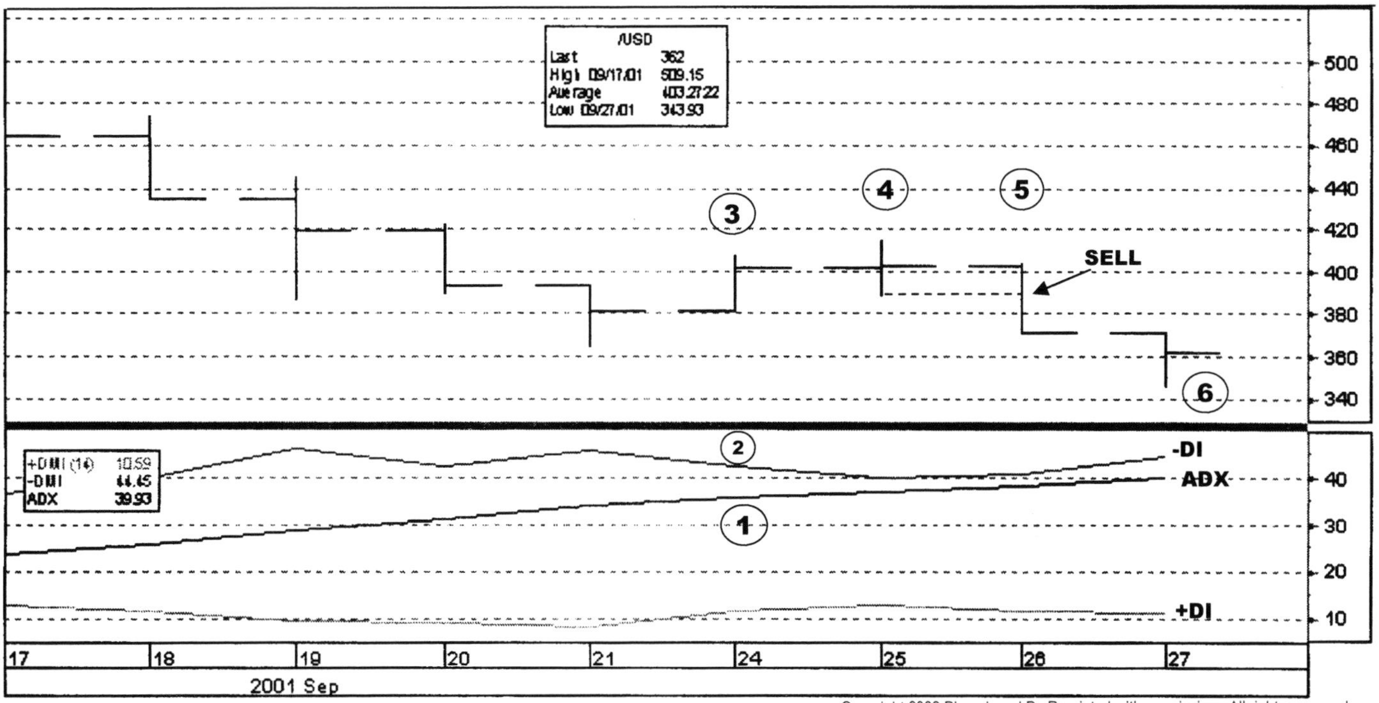

/USD
Last 362
High 09/17/01 509.15
Average 403.2722
Low 09/27/01 343.93

500
480
460
440
420
400
380
360
340

3
4
5
SELL
6

+DMI (14) 10.59
-DMI 44.45
ADX 39.93

2
-DI
ADX
1
+DI

40
30
20
10

17 18 19 20 21 24 25 26 27

2001 Sep

Here is an example with the Semis.

1. The ADX is above 25, signifying a strong trend.

2. The -DI is greater than the +DI, telling us the trend is down.

3. A close in the top 25% of the range.

4. Pause day.

5. We get a sell signal just under the pause day low.

6. A better than 6.5% move in a day.

As you can see, this method is simple and easy to identify. Here is the catch: Most of the trigger days will never trigger. You must be patient and wait for the trigger to occur. This is one of the keys.

Let's now look at a few examples using 20-day highs and 20-day lows.

Example 6 — Semiconductor Index (SOX)

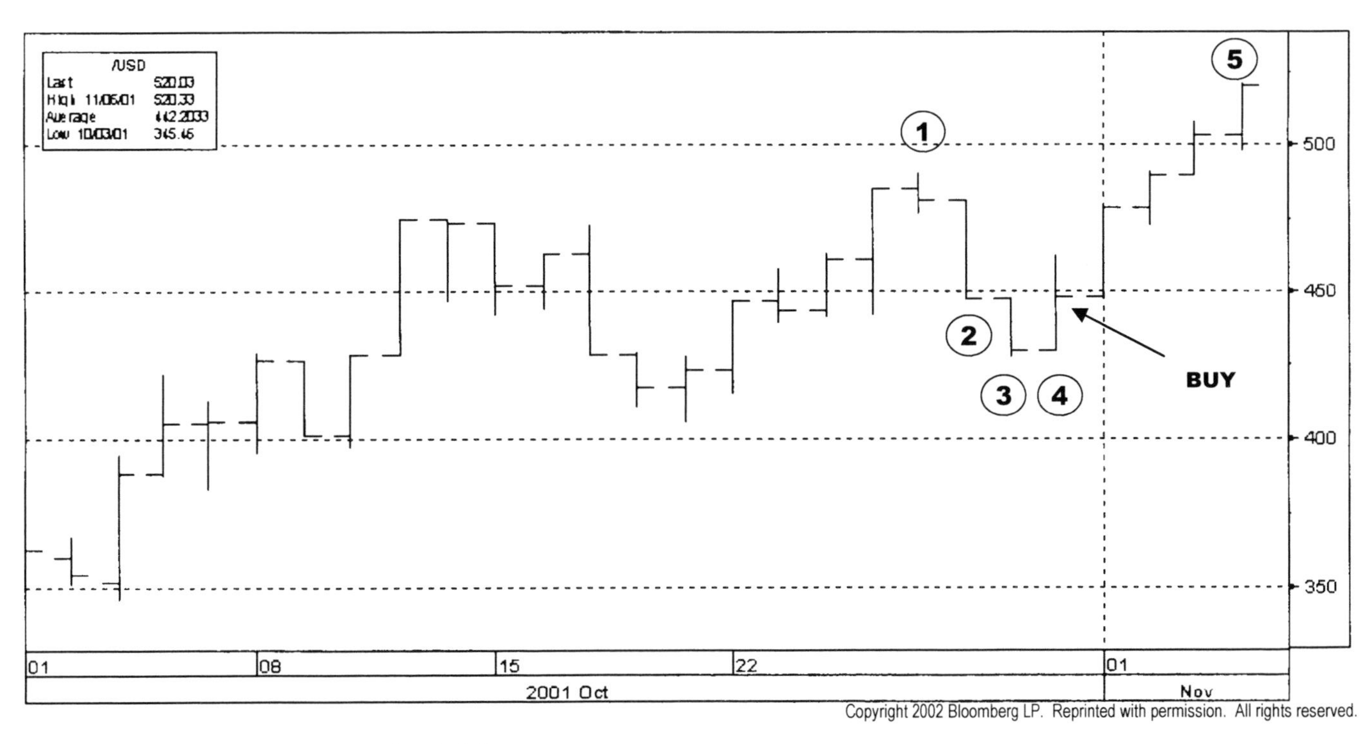

1. 20-day high.
2. Close in the bottom 25% of the range.
3. Pause day.
4. Buy.
5. Four straight up days in a row.

Example 7 — S&P 500 Index (SPX)

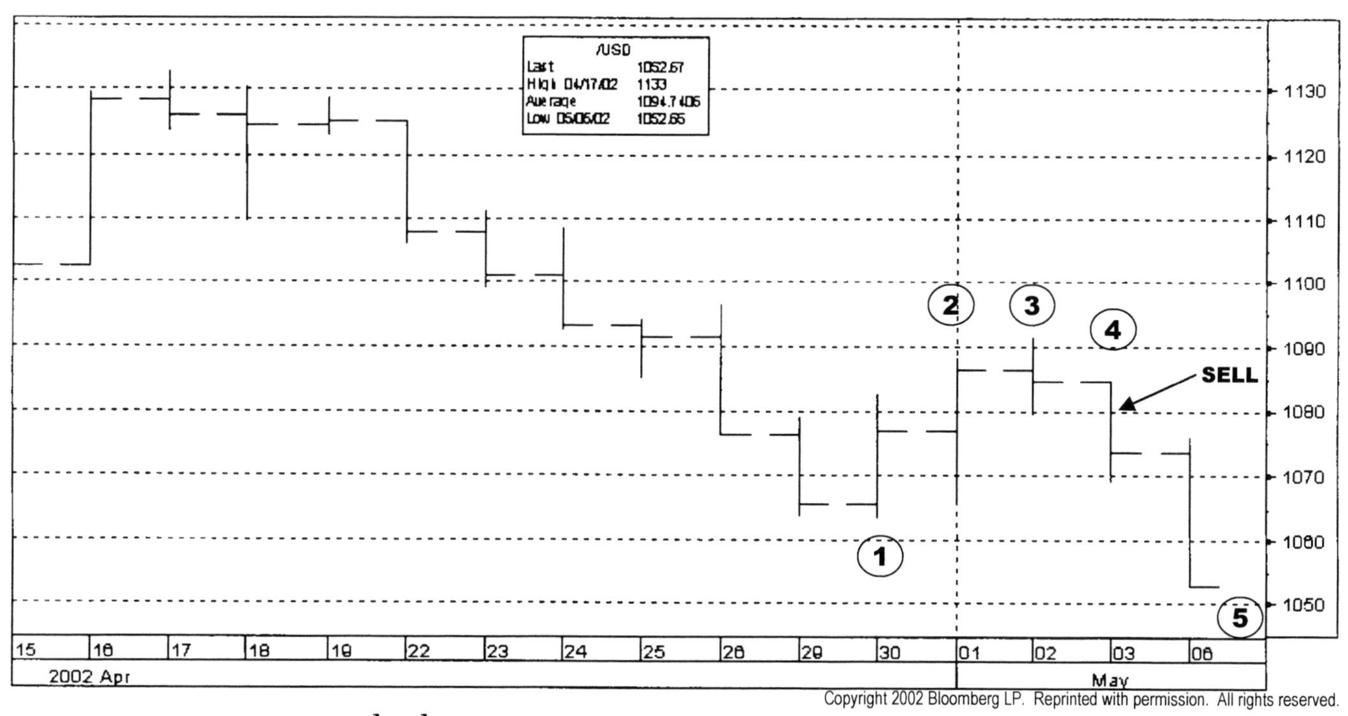

1. 20-day low.
2. Close in the top 25% of the range.
3. Pause day.
4. Sell at 1079.46.
5. Collapses to 1052.67 the next day.

Part Three
The Markets and Stocks To Focus On

Because this is a few hours to a few days setup, you must be in markets and stocks that move! To be effective, these markets must have larger than normal daily ranges. That means not trading markets such as utilities, REITs, or stocks with small daily ranges! Even the S&Ps are not fully volatile enough sometimes to trade this. Which markets and stocks should you focus on? The most volatile are the Nasdaq stocks and the higher-priced stocks in the Semiconductor Index (SOX). The QQQs and the SMHs are also good, followed by the brokerage stocks. The more volatile the market, the bigger the risk. But this is where the biggest moves occur. And when the trend resumes, you can get some very substantial gains.

Now let's quickly look at some statistical evidence. Here are the results from the Nasdaq 100, the SOX and the XBDs (Brokerage Index) using ADX as the filter.

TradeStation Strategy Performance Report
NDX - Daily (1/2/91-4/25/02)
AS OF THE CLOSE ON THE DAY OF ENTRY

Performance Summary: All Trades

Total Net Profit	857.66 points	Open position P/L	0.00
Gross Profit	2,281.59	Gross Loss	(1,423.93)
Total # of trades	142	Percent profitable	61.27%
Number winning trades	87	Number losing trades	55
Largest winning trade	163.99	Largest losing trade	(189.00)
Average winning trade	26.23	Average losing trade	(25.89)
Ratio avg win/avg loss	1.01	Avg trade (win & loss)	6.04
Max consec. Winners	8	Max consec. losers	4
Avg # bars in winners	0	Avg # bars in losers	0
Max intraday drawdown	(377.10)		
Profit Factor	1.60	Max # contracts held	1
Account size required	377.10	Return on account	227.44%

Performance Summary: Long Trades

Total Net Profit	584.50	Open position P/L	0.00
Gross Profit	1,062.34	Gross Loss	(477.84)
Total # of trades	85	Percent profitable	67.06%
Number winning trades	57	Number losing trades	28
Largest winning trade	159.00	Largest losing trade	(142.00)
Average winning trade	18.64	Average losing trade	(17.07)
Ratio avg win/avg loss	1.09	Avg trade (win & loss)	6.88
Max consec. Winners	8	Max consec. losers	4
Avg # bars in winners	0	Avg # bars in losers	0
Max intraday drawdown	(209.00)		
Profit Factor	2.22	Max # contracts held	1
Account size required	209.00	Return on account	279.67%

Performance Summary: Short Trades

Total Net Profit 273.16		Open position P/L	0.00
Gross Profit	1,219.25	Gross Loss	(946.09)
Total # of trades	57	Percent profitable	52.63%
Number winning trades	30	Number losing trades	27
Largest winning trade	163.99	Largest losing trade	(189.00)
Average winning trade	40.64	Average losing trade	(35.04)
Ratio avg win/avg loss	1.16	Avg trade (win & loss)	4.79
Max consec. Winners	6	Max consec. losers	6
Avg # bars in winners	0	Avg # bars in losers	0
Max intraday drawdown	(306.08)		
Profit Factor	1.29	Max # contracts held	1
Account size required	306.08	Return on account	89.24%

TradeStation Strategy Performance Report
NDX - Daily (1/2/91-4/25/02)
NEXT-DAY EXIT

Performance Summary: All Trades

Total Net Profit	1,154.20 points	Open position P/L	0.00
Gross Profit	3,481.31	Gross Loss	(2,327.11)
Total # of trades	134	Percent profitable	51.49%
Number winning trades	69	Number losing trades	65
Largest winning trade	290.99	Largest losing trade	(192.00)
Average winning trade	50.45	Average losing trade	(35.80)
Ratio avg win/avg loss	1.41	Avg trade (win & loss)	8.61
Max consec. Winners	6	Max consec. losers	5
Avg # bars in winners	1	Avg # bars in losers	1
Max intraday drawdown	(338.06)		
Profit Factor	1.50	Max # contracts held	1
Account size required	338.06	Return on account	341.42%

Performance Summary: Long Trades

Total Net Profit	658.84	Open position P/L	0.00
Gross Profit	1,314.76	Gross Loss	(655.92)
Total # of trades	78	Percent profitable	55.13%
Number winning trades	43	Number losing trades	35
Largest winning trade	155.99	Largest losing trade	(142.01)
Average winning trade	30.58	Average losing trade	(18.74)
Ratio avg win/avg loss	1.63	Avg trade (win & loss)	8.45
Max consec. Winners	6	Max consec. losers	4
Avg # bars in winners	1	Avg # bars in losers	1
Max intraday drawdown	(209.01)		
Profit Factor	2.00	Max # contracts held	1
Account size required	209.01	Return on account	315.22%

Performance Summary: Short Trades

Total Net Profit	495.36	Open position P/L	0.00
Gross Profit	2,166.55	Gross Loss	(1,671.19)
Total # of trades	56	Percent profitable	46.43%
Number winning trades	26	Number losing trades	30
Largest winning trade	290.99	Largest losing trade	(192.00)
Average winning trade	83.33	Average losing trade	(55.71)
Ratio avg win/avg loss	1.50	Avg trade (win & loss)	8.85
Max consec. Winners	4	Max consec. losers	4
Avg # bars in winners	1	Avg # bars in losers	1

You gained more NDX points with the 1-Day Breakout Method than Buy-and-Hold did in 11 years!

TradeStation Strategy Performance Report
SOX - Daily (5/4/94-4/25/02)
SAME-DAY EXIT

Performance Summary: All Trades

Total Net Profit	432.19 points	Open position P/L	0.00
Gross Profit	801.93	Gross Loss	(369.74)
Total # of trades	113	Percent profitable	70.80%
Number winning trades	80	Number losing trades	33
Largest winning trade	100.71	Largest losing trade	(74.71)
Average winning trade	10.02	Average losing trade	(11.20)
Ratio avg win/avg loss	.89	Avg trade (win & loss)	3.82
Max consec. Winners	11	Max consec. losers	3
Avg # bars in winners	0	Avg # bars in losers	0
Max intraday drawdown	(186.16)		
Profit Factor	2.17	Max # contracts held	1
Account size required	186.16	Return on account	232.16%

Performance Summary: Long Trades

Total Net Profit	379.62	Open position P/L	0.00
Gross Profit	445.13	Gross Loss	(65.51)
Total # of trades	70	Percent profitable	77.14%
Number winning trades	54	Number losing trades	16
Largest winning trade	100.71	Largest losing trade	(23.74)
Average winning trade	8.24	Average losing trade	(4.09)
Ratio avg win/avg loss	2.01	Avg trade (win & loss)	5.42
Max consec. Winners	11	Max consec. losers	2
Avg # bars in winners	0	Avg # bars in losers	0
Max intraday drawdown	(27.00)		
Profit Factor	6.79	Max # contracts held	1
Account size required	27.00	Return on account	1406.00%

Performance Summary: Short Trades

Total Net Profit	52.57	Open position P/L	0.00
Gross Profit	356.80	Gross Loss	(304.23)
Total # of trades	43	Percent profitable	60.47%
Number winning trades	26	Number losing trades	17
Largest winning trade	63.29	Largest losing trade	(74.71)
Average winning trade	13.72	Average losing trade	(17.90)
Ratio avg win/avg loss	.77	Avg trade (win & loss)	1.22
Max consec. Winners	4	Max consec. losers	3
Avg # bars in winners	0	Avg # bars in losers	0
Max intraday drawdown	(186.16)		
Profit Factor	1.17	Max # contracts held	1
Account size required	186.16	Return on account	28.24%

Performance tables created with TradeStation2000i by TradeStation Technologies, Inc. TradeStation is a registered trademark of TradeStation Technologies, Inc.

TradeStation Strategy Performance Report
SOX - Daily (5/4/94-4/25/02)
NEXT-DAY EXIT

Performance Summary: All Trades

Total Net Profit	702.72 points	Open position P/L	0.00
Gross Profit	1,190.43	Gross Loss	(487.71)
Total # of trades	109	Percent profitable	62.39%
Number winning trades	68	Number losing trades	41
Largest winning trade	130.04	Largest losing trade	(81.52)
Average winning trade	17.51	Average losing trade	(11.90)
Ratio avg win/avg loss	1.47	Avg trade (win & loss)	6.45
Max consec. Winners	15	Max consec. losers	9
Avg # bars in winners	1	Avg # bars in losers	1
Max intraday drawdown	(144.45)		
Profit Factor	2.44	Max # contracts held	1
Account size required	144.45	Return on account	486.48%

Performance Summary: Long Trades

Total Net Profit	435.24	Open position P/L	0.00
Gross Profit	557.13	Gross Loss	(121.89)
Total # of trades	66	Percent profitable	66.67%
Number winning trades	44	Number losing trades	22
Largest winning trade	102.43	Largest losing trade	(32.62)
Average winning trade	12.66	Average losing trade	(5.54)
Ratio avg win/avg loss	2.29	Avg trade (win & loss)	6.59
Max consec. Winners	15	Max consec. losers	8
Avg # bars in winners	1	Avg # bars in losers	1
Max intraday drawdown	(57.85)		
Profit Factor	4.57	Max # contracts held	1
Account size required	57.85	Return on account	752.36%

Performance Summary: Short Trades

Total Net Profit	267.48	Open position P/L	0.00
Gross Profit	633.30	Gross Loss	(365.82)
Total # of trades	43	Percent profitable	55.81%
Number winning trades	24	Number losing trades	19
Largest winning trade	130.04	Largest losing trade	(81.52)
Average winning trade	26.39	Average losing trade	(19.25)
Ratio avg win/avg loss	1.37	Avg trade (win & loss)	6.22

Same story as the Nasdaq. The ODBM gave you more points since inception of the SOX with the 1-day hold than the market achieved over an eight-year period!

TradeStation Strategy Performance Report
XBD - Daily (4/15/94-4/25/02)
SAME-DAY EXIT

Performance Summary: All Trades

Total Net Profit	276.79 points	Open position P/L	0.00
Gross Profit	453.16	Gross Loss	(176.37)
Total # of trades	138	Percent profitable	75.36%
Number winning trades	104	Number losing trades	34
Largest winning trade	33.74	Largest losing trade	(36.09)
Average winning trade	4.36	Average losing trade	(5.19)
Ratio avg win/avg loss	.84	Avg trade (win & loss)	2.01
Max consec. Winners	15	Max consec. losers	3
Avg # bars in winners	0	Avg # bars in losers	0
Max intraday drawdown	(44.30)		
Profit Factor	2.57	Max # contracts held	1
Account size required	44.30	Return on account	624.81%

Performance Summary: Long Trades

Total Net Profit	218.07	Open position P/L	0.00
Gross Profit	320.74	Gross Loss	(102.67)
Total # of trades	101	Percent profitable	77.23%
Number winning trades	78	Number losing trades	23
Largest winning trade	33.74	Largest losing trade	(16.08)
Average winning trade	4.11	Average losing trade	(4.46)
Ratio avg win/avg loss	.92	Avg trade (win & loss)	2.16
Max consec. Winners	15	Max consec. losers	2
Avg # bars in winners	0	Avg # bars in losers	0
Max intraday drawdown	(25.16)		
Profit Factor	3.12	Max # contracts held	1
Account size required	25.16	Return on account	866.73%

Performance Summary: Short Trades

Total Net Profit	58.72	Open position P/L	0.00
Gross Profit	132.42	Gross Loss	(73.70)
Total # of trades	37	Percent profitable	70.27%
Number winning trades	26	Number losing trades	11
Largest winning trade	24.12	Largest losing trade	(36.09)
Average winning trade	5.09	Average losing trade	(6.70)
Ratio avg win/avg loss	.76	Avg trade (win & loss)	1.59
Max consec. Winners	7	Max consec. losers	2
Avg # bars in winners	0	Avg # bars in losers	0

Look at the percent correct circled above!

TradeStation Strategy Performance Report
XBD - Daily (4/15/94-4/25/02)
NEXT-DAY EXIT

Performance Summary: All Trades

Total Net Profit	432.33 points	Open position P/L	0.00
Gross Profit	634.94	Gross Loss	(202.61)
Total # of trades	126	Percent profitable	66.67%
Number winning trades	84	Number losing trades	42
Largest winning trade	38.05	Largest losing trade	(37.90)
Average winning trade	7.56	Average losing trade	(4.82)
Ratio avg win/avg loss	1.57	Avg trade (win & loss)	3.43
Max consec. Winners	11	Max consec. losers	5
Avg # bars in winners	1	Avg # bars in losers	1
Max intraday drawdown	(51.12)		
Profit Factor	3.13	Max # contracts held	1
Account size required	51.12	Return on account	845.72%

Performance Summary: Long Trades

Total Net Profit	293.64	Open position P/L	0.00
Gross Profit	415.13	Gross Loss	(121.49)
Total # of trades	92	Percent profitable	65.22%
Number winning trades	60	Number losing trades	32
Largest winning trade	37.20	Largest losing trade	(23.01)
Average winning trade	6.92	Average losing trade	(3.80)
Ratio avg win/avg loss	1.82	Avg trade (win & loss)	3.19
Max consec. Winners	11	Max consec. losers	5
Avg # bars in winners	1	Avg # bars in losers	1
Max intraday drawdown	(51.12)		
Profit Factor	3.42	Max # contracts held	1
Account size required	51.12	Return on account	574.41%

Performance Summary: Short Trades

Total Net Profit	138.69	Open position P/L	0.00
Gross Profit	219.81	Gross Loss	(81.12)
Total # of trades	34	Percent profitable	70.59%
Number winning trades	24	Number losing trades	10
Largest winning trade	38.05	Largest losing trade	(37.90)
Average winning trade	9.16	Average losing trade	(8.11)
Ratio avg win/avg loss	1.13	Avg trade (win & loss)	4.08
Max consec. Winners	6	Max consec. losers	2
Avg # bars in winners	1	Avg # bars in losers	1
Max intraday drawdown	(40.87)		
Profit Factor	2.71	Max # contracts held	1
Account size required	40.87	Return on account	339.34%

As you can see, the results are quite extraordinary. And the results using 20-day new highs and new lows are not far different.

What also stands out is the fact that the method has made money on both the long side and on the short side. Too many methods are "bull market only" methods, but that is not the case here. As you can see, the setups were profitable both on the buy side and the short side.

As mentioned earlier, the results have killed Buy-and-Hold. From May 1994 (the start of the SOX Index) through April 2002, the SOX rose 396 points had you been in it the entire time. **With the ODBM method, you were out of the market a little higher than 91% of the time! Yet, with the one-day hold, you earned 702 points!**

Now, let's look at the XBDs. From April 1994 (the start of the index) through April 2002, the XBDs rose 397 points. **With our method, you were in the market only 10.6% of the time and earned 432 points!**

As for the Nasdaq, it rose 1050 points from January 1991 – April 2002. With the ODBM method, you were only in the market 7.7% of the time (out of the market 92.3%), yet you earned more!

The rewards have been far greater, and the risk has been far less, trading the ODBM vs. Buy-And-Hold and many other trading methods. The key here is to be able to identify the times the market is trending strongly and climb aboard after a quick reversal. The results above are no guarantee that this will continue in the future. But they do show the evidence of the method in action.

The above analysis is not as important as the average profit per trade this method gives you. And as you can see, the average profit per trade for the SOX is high. This is because of the SOX's volatility. The average profit per trade after one day for the S&Ps is under 3 points. That is because it is far less volatile than the SOX. **Stick with large-range securities and markets to maximize the effectiveness of the ODBM.**

The final point of the analysis is critical to understand. This is

a method that takes lots and lots of small gains and small losses. Then, you get one very large move, and this is where your profits will come from. This is very important to remember. Keep your stops in place to protect yourself and to keep the losses to a minimum. And understand that the gains will come from one out of every six to eight trades.

Money Management

Again, this is not a mechanical method. Initial protective stops need to be in place. This means upon being filled, place a stop in case you are wrong. The stop can raise from the mid-point of yesterday's bar to the bottom of yesterday's bar (for short sells it would be the top of yesterday's bar). Your exit can be at the close or at the close on half your position and let the other half carry overnight. Ideally, you want the next day to move in your favor immediately and keep moving your stops up (down for shorts) as the market runs. There is no way of telling how far the move will go. **Remember, you are on the same side of the trend, and there will be times that the market explodes in your favor as trending markets do.** Your exit strategy should be dependent upon your risk parameters and your trading style. Only you know what's best for you. The most important thing is to use protective stops upon entering the position and then trail your stops as the position becomes profitable.

Another method to look at is the 2-for-1 Money Management method. Let's assume you buy a stock at 50 and your stop is at 49 (1 point). You will take profits on half your position on what you originally risked (1 point) at 51 and raise your stop on the other half to your original buy point. This guarantees (barring something crazy happening intraday or overnight) that you will have a profitable trade. As the position continues to move in your favor, you keep moving your stop up closer and closer on your remaining position until your profits are locked in.

Q&A

What is the most obvious characteristic of the ODBM?

Answer: The most obvious characteristic of this method is that it gives you a lot of small gains and small losses. One out of every six to eight trades gives you a very large trend-following move and these moves can be substantial. The key is to be there for the move. One never knows when it will occur, but trend explosions are a part of the makeup of the strategy.

Which is better to use, ADX or 20-day new highs/lows?

Answer: ADX is a bit stronger, but they are both good.

How do I enter the positions? Do I have to be in front of the screen all day?

Answer: No. You can identify the potential setups the night before. Then, before the market opens, you can place your buy stop or sell-short stops in. Should you get filled, then you can place your initial protective stops.

How do I find the setups?

Answer: Two ways:

1. You can do it by hand
2. You can use a software program (See Appendix)

Is there any best market or stock to trade?

Answer: Yes. The more volatile the market and stock, the greater the potential move. Remember, you are likely taking many small losses and small gains along the way and you want to be in the ones that will explode or implode the most when the correct move occurs.

One can't trade the NDX, SOX or XBDs. What can be traded?

Answer: These indicies can be traded with their derivatives. The NDX can be traded with the Nasdaq 100 Trust (QQQ), or the Nasdaq or E-Mini Nasdaq futures. The SOX can be traded with the Semiconductor HLDRs (SMH), and the XBDs can be traded with the iShares. The symbol is IYG. Also, you can trade the individual stocks in these groups, especially the higher-priced, more volatile ones.

You show results that use a 1-day exit. Is that the best way to trade this?

Answer: It can be. It depends upon your trading style. But if you are a good trader, you will likely get even higher results by using trailing stops instead of a mechanical exit. This is a personal choice that you can decide upon.

Conclusion

As you can see, this is a very simple system to follow. And it has historically proven to provide a very large edge. You will be looking for markets that are strongly trending, that close poorly, then pause, and reverse the next day in the direction of the trend. Ideally, you will look for the stocks and markets that have the biggest range and volatility as you will only be in a position for a few days. Stops near the opposite end of yesterday's range will provide you with some protection from intraday reversals. Trailing stops and/or the 2-for-1 money management method will help you lock into the gains as they occur.

We wish you the best of luck trading the 1-Day Breakout Method!

Software Add-on Module

for Omega Research TradeStation and SuperCharts users

1-Day Breakout Method Add-on Module for Omega Research TradeStation and SuperCharts Users by Gregory Che

Owners of Omega Research TradeStation v. 4.0, 2000i, and 6.0 or SuperCharts 4.0 are able to purchase and install a Strategy and a ShowMe Study for both the ADX– and New High/New Low-based versions of the 1-Day Breakout Method. The Strategies will allow you to back-test the 1-Day Breakout Method on different markets, and the ShowMe study will clearly define all the steps that lead to a 1-Day Breakout Method setup.

This add-on will also allow you to automatically scan (TradeStation v. 4.0, 2000i and SuperCharts 4.0 users only) for setups nightly on a universe of stocks you have downloaded data for. This scan will also produce a printable list of potential setups for the next trading day. TradeStation 6.0 users will be able to manually scroll through a set of stocks or markets and the program will automatically highlight those that are setting up for a potential trade the next day.

3.5" Floppy Disk and Complete Installation and Usage Instructions Included

$75.00

Call **1-888-484-8220 x1**

Or

Go To **www.TradersGalleria.com**

to order your copy today!!